THE KREGEL PICTORIAL GUIDE TO THE TABERNACLE

kregel
PUBLICATIONS

Grand Rapids, MI   49501

© 2002 Angus Hudson Ltd/
Tim Dowley & Peter Wyart dba
Three's Company

Published by Kregel Publications,
a division of Kregel, Inc., P.O. Box
2607, Grand Rapids, MI 49501.
Kregel Publications provides
trusted, biblical publications for
Christian growth and service. Your
comments and suggestions are
valued.

ISBN 978-0-8254-2468-7

Designed by Peter Wyart

Worldwide coedition organized
and produced by
Angus Hudson Ltd.
Concorde House, Grenville Place,
Mill Hill, London NW7 3SA,
England
Tel: +44 20 8959 3668
Fax +44 20 8959 3678

Printed in Singapore

PICTURE ACKNOWLEDGMENTS

Photographs
Bible Museum, Amsterdam: pp. 15
  (bottom left), 28 (bottom)
Tim Dowley: pp. 5, 11, 18 (top), 18
  (bottom), 32
Roger Eyre, with thanks to the
  Tabernacle Project Team: p. 23
Hanan Isaachar: pp. 6, 14, 15 (top
  right), 17 (bottom), 19
Israel Government Tourist Office:
  pp. 24, 27 (top, Sa'ar Ya'acov)
Gerth Medien, Asslar, Germany:
  pp. 1, 4–5, 14 (inset)
Zev Radovan: pp. 16 (bottom), 17
  (top), 21 (bottom), 22 (both)
Peter Wyart: p. 28 (top)

Illustrations
Alan Parry: pp. 3, 20–21, 30–31
Richard Scott: pp. 12, 25

Contents

The Tabernacle – God's Tent   4

Three Tabernacles   6

The History of the Tabernacle:
The Wilderness Years   8

The History of the Tabernacle:
Into the Promised Land   10

The Structure of the Tabernacle   12

The Furniture of the Tabernacle:
The Most Holy Place   15

The Furniture of the Tabernacle:
The Holy Place   17

The Outer Courtyard and its Furniture   20

Making and Moving the Tabernacle   23

The Sacrifices of the Temple   24

The Levites and priests   25

Holy Days and Festivals   26

The Symbolism of the Tabernacle   29

Solomon's Temple   30

What Happened to the Ark?   32

Index   32

The Tabernacle—God's Tent

About fifty chapters of the Bible are concerned with the tabernacle, indicating its importance in the development of the religious life of Israel.

Why the tabernacle?
The tabernacle was a portable sanctuary—a holy place for worshipping God—created in the desert in response to the demand for mobility. It symbolized God's presence with his people, and was a place where his will was communicated.

At this time the people of Israel were journeying from Egypt through the wilderness toward the Promised Land, and they were living in tents, so the tabernacle was also a tent. It was designed so that it could easily be dismantled when the Israelites moved their camp and reassembled at the next halting place.

The tabernacle and the temple

The Israelites anticipated that once peace and security had been attained, a permanent national shrine would be set up (Deut. 12:10–11). However, this was not realized until the time of King Solomon, when the first temple was erected (2 Sam. 7:10–13; 1 Kings 5:1–5). The tabernacle was thus a forerunner of the temple.

The tabernacle and temple are closely linked both historically and by their similarity in construction and underlying theology.

How we know about the tabernacle

The fullest and most reliable source of information about the tabernacle is the Bible, especially the book of Exodus. Exodus 25–28 prescribes the construction and furniture of the tabernacle, while Exodus 35–40 describes how it was made. We are also helped by the specifications for Solomon's temple (1 Kings 6; 2 Chronicles 3–4), and the temple seen in a vision by the prophet Ezekiel (Ezekiel 40–43), both of which followed the basic plan of the tabernacle.

An artist's impression of the tabernacle in the wilderness near Mount Sinai. Notice the camp of Israel is set up around the central tabernacle.

Three Tabernacles

The Old Testament mentions three tabernacles:

1. The provisional tabernacle or Tent of Meeting
This was established after the Israelites sinned by setting up and worshiping a golden calf at Mount Sinai (Ex. 32:1–33:6). Probably Moses' own tent, it was pitched outside the camp to symbolize the departure of God from among the people as punishment for their sin. This "tent for meeting with God" had no ritual and no priesthood. Joshua was its only attendant, and the Jewish people consulted it as an oracle (Ex. 33:7).

The view from Mount Sinai, sometimes known as Mount Moses.

A full-scale replica of the tabernacle has been set up in the Negev, Israel.

2. The Sinai tabernacle

This tabernacle is first mentioned in Exodus 25:8, where God says to Moses, "Then have them make a sanctuary for me, and I will dwell among them." It was erected according to the directions given to Moses by God. We discuss this in detail later in this book.

3. David's tabernacle

This tabernacle was erected by David in his new capital city, Jerusalem, to receive the Ark of the Covenant (2 Sam. 6:12–17). The old tabernacle and its bronze altar apparently stayed at Gibeon until the days of King Solomon, and remained the place where sacrifices were offered (1 Chron. 16:39; 2 Chron. 1:3).

Portable temples

The tabernacle and temple were made up of three distinct zones: a general area and two restricted areas. This was a common arrangement in temples in the ancient Middle East; excavations of heathen sanctuaries in Palestine and Syria from the pre-Israelite period have revealed many similarly divided sanctuaries.

Portable prefabricated structures were in widespread use during the second millennium B.C. In addition to their use as portable religious sanctuaries, they served as portable staterooms for kings and other high dignitaries. Rulers in both Egypt and Canaan used such structures when travelling to different parts of their kingdoms. Nomadic and semi-nomadic peoples, such as the Midianites, also used portable sanctuaries.

Names for the Tabernacle

The tabernacle of Israel was known by several different Hebrew terms.

Sanctuary
(Ex. 25:8; 38:24; Lev. 12:4)
The English word *sanctuary* was used to translate two Hebrew words, both meaning "holy, consecrated place"—one of the words (*qodesh*) comes from the Hebrew verb *to be holy*. These two words applied both to the whole structure (Lev. 4:6; Num. 3:38, 4:12) and to its innermost sanctuary, the Most Holy Place, often known as the Holy of Holies (Lev. 16:2).

Tent
The single word *tent* (Hebrew, *ohel*) occurs nineteen times. The word is also found in expressions such as "the Tent of the Testimony" (Num. 9:15), a name derived from the two tablets of stone containing the Ten Commandments, or "Testimony," that were kept inside the Ark of the Covenant within the tabernacle (Ex. 25:16, 21; 31:18).

The tabernacle was also known as "the tent of the LORD" (1 Kings 2:28–30), 'the house called the Tent" (1 Chron. 9:23), and "the Tent of Meeting"—literally, the tent "where I meet with you" (see, for example, Ex. 29:42, 44; 33:7; Num. 17:4). This last phrase occurs about 130 times in the Bible, underlining that the tabernacle was the place where God met with Moses and his people to make known his will.

Dwelling
(Ex. 25:9; 26:1)
The Hebrew word *miskan*, meaning "dwelling," is the word translated "tabernacle" in the NIV. It is connected with the Jewish (but not biblical) word *Shekinah*, describing the dwelling place of the divine glory. In Exodus 25:9 the word means the "whole tabernacle," but in Exodus 26:1 it refers to the Holy Place and the Most Holy Place. A similar phrase, "the tabernacle [dwelling] of the testimony" (Ex. 38:21), emphasizes the presence of the tablets of the Law in the tabernacle.

House
(Ex. 23:19; 34:26)
The phrase the "house of the Lord" conveys the idea of a fixed dwelling. For this reason it was more appropriate to the stationary tabernacle set up after the Jewish people settled in Canaan, than to the mobile tabernacle of their wilderness wanderings.

Temple
(1 Sam. 1:9; 3:3)
The Hebrew word for "temple" also means "palace"; the temple was God's palace (compare 1 Chron. 29:1, 19). This word was used of the later tabernacles at Shiloh (1 Sam. 1:9; 3:3) and Jerusalem (Ps. 5:7).

The History of the Tabernacle
The wilderness years

It was at Mount Sinai, today identified with Jebel Musa, at the base of which stands St. Catherine's Monastery, that Moses received the Law. When the Jews turned from God and started to worship the golden calf in the wilderness, Moses angrily shattered the tablets of stone inscribed with the Ten Commandments. After the people repented, Moses climbed Mount Sinai again to intercede with God.

Constructing the tabernacle
God renewed his covenant with Israel, gave them a second copy of the Law, and invited them to offer materials with which to construct the tabernacle. The people responded generously, and gave much more than was needed (Ex. 36:5-6); the work went ahead under the direction of Bezalel and Oholiab (Ex. 35:30; 36:2).

The tabernacle was completed on the first day of the first Jewish month (Abib, March-April) in the second year after the exodus from Egypt. The cycle of sacrifices and worship that God had laid down for the new sanctuary now began (Ex. 40:2).

The tabernacle in the camp
Unlike the provisional tabernacle (see p. 6), this permanent tabernacle stood in the very center of the Jewish encampment. It must have appeared very impressive, with Mount Sinai as its backdrop. Moses and Aaron set up their tents on the east side of the tabernacle, and the other three families of priests on the other three sides—the family of Kohath to the south; the family of Gershon on the west; the family of Merari on the north—acting as the "bodyguard" of Israel's ruler, God. This prevented any unauthorized intrusion into the sacred area. This pattern is still followed by tent-dwellers in the Middle East. In a Bedouin camp the chieftain's tent occupies a central position with the families grouped around it in their allotted positions.

Outside the inner square, in a wider square, the tribes of Judah, Zebulun, and Issachar camped on the eastern side under the standard of Judah; Ephraim, Manasseh, and Benjamin to the west under the standard of Ephraim; the less conspicuous tribes, Dan, Asher, and Naphtali to the north under the standard of Dan; Reuben, Simeon and Gad on the south side under the standard of Reuben.

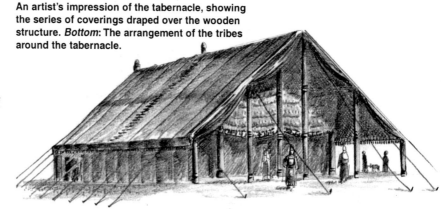

An artist's impression of the tabernacle, showing the series of coverings draped over the wooden structure. *Bottom*: The arrangement of the tribes around the tabernacle.

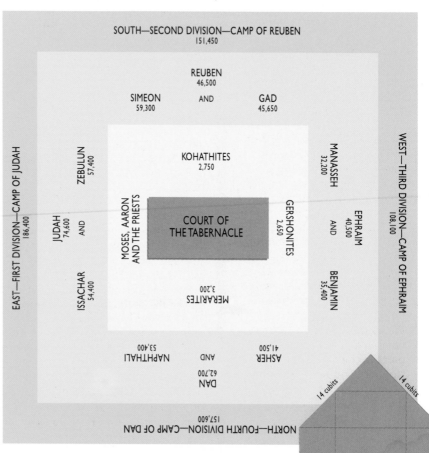

SOUTH—SECOND DIVISION—CAMP OF REUBEN
151,450

REUBEN 46,500

SIMEON 59,300   AND   GAD 45,650

EAST—FIRST DIVISION—CAMP OF JUDAH

ZEBULUN 57,400

JUDAH 74,600   AND

ISSACHAR 54,400

KOHATHITES 2,750

MOSES, AARON AND THE PRIESTS

COURT OF THE TABERNACLE

GERSHONITES 2,650

MERARITES 3,200

MANASSEH 32,200

EPHRAIM 40,500   AND

BENJAMIN 35,400

WEST—THIRD DIVISION—CAMP OF EPHRAIM
108,100

NAPHTALI 53,400   AND

DAN 62,700

ASHER 41,500

NORTH—FOURTH DIVISION—CAMP OF DAN
157,600

14 cubits   14 cubits

The Exodus

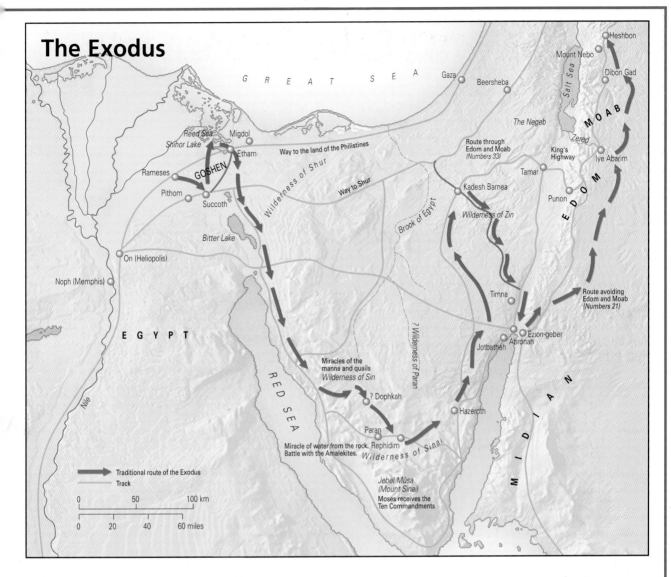

Map labels:
GREAT SEA
Gaza · Beersheba
The Negeb
Heshbon · Mount Nebo · Dibon Gad · MOAB · Zered · Iye Abarim
Salt Sea
Route through Edom and Moab *(Numbers 33)*
King's Highway
Tamar · EDOM · Punon
Kadesh Barnea · *Wilderness of Zin*
Reed Sea · Shihor Lake · Migdol · Etham
Way to the land of the Philistines
Rameses · GOSHEN · Pithom · Succoth
Wilderness of Shur · Way to Shur
Brook of Egypt
Bitter Lake
On (Heliopolis)
Noph (Memphis)
EGYPT
Nile
RED SEA
Timna
? Wilderness of Paran
Route avoiding Edom and Moab *(Numbers 21)*
Ezion-geber · Abronah · Jotbathah
MIDIAN
Miracles of the manna and quails *Wilderness of Sin*
? Dophkah
Hazeroth
Paran
Miracle of water from the rock. Battle with the Amalekites. Rephidim
Wilderness of Sinai
Jebel Mūsa (Mount Sinai) Moses receives the Ten Commandments

Legend:
Traditional route of the Exodus
Track
0   50   100 km
0 20 40 60 miles

A nineteenth-century engraving of Mount Sinai, or Mount Horeb.

Breaking camp
The Israelites remained at the foot of Mount Sinai for a year, until the tabernacle and its furnishings were completed. Then they set out again, heading for the Promised Land (Num. 10:11). When the Israelite army organized the people for the march, the tabernacle, carried on the shoulders of Levites, remained at the center, with the tribes from the east and south sides of the camp marching in front of it, those from the north and west to the rear (Numbers 2).

En route
Although the Bible records the route taken by the Israelites in the wilderness, most of the places named in the itinerary in Numbers 33 are today unknown. Two sites can be definitely identified: Hazeroth and Kadesh. Hazeroth has usually been identified with Ein Hudra, an oasis west of the Red Sea. Kadesh-Barnea is today usually identified with the valley of Ein el-Qudeirat, a lush oasis based around the biggest spring in the

area. It is situated in northern Sinai at the crossroads of two major routes across the desert, a site surveyed by the British archaeologist Leonard Woolley and T. E. Lawrence – "Lawrence of Arabia"—just before World War I.

Rebellion in the camp

The Israelites arrived at Kadesh nearly a year after leaving Sinai, and it was from here that Moses sent out twelve spies to reconnoiter the Promised Land (Num. 13). When all the spies except Joshua and Caleb returned with discouraging reports, the Israelites panicked. Their fear turned to fury, and there was a mass uprising. Moses' and Aaron's lives were saved only by the direct intervention of God at the tabernacle (Num. 14:1–10). Because of their failure to trust God, the Israelites were condemned to remain in the wilderness until all the adults who had left Egypt had died (Num. 14:20–25).

A fresh start

It was thirty-eight years before the Israelites, with the tabernacle in their midst, again set out for the Promised Land. After leaving Kadesh-Barnea, circling around Edom, and defeating the Amorites and Og King of Bashan, they encamped on the Plains of Moab (Num. 33:48–49) at the oasis formed by springs in the foothills of Moab. From here, Moses climbed mount Pisgah (also known as Nebo; Deut. 34:1) to look at the Promised Land, which he was not to be permitted to enter (Deut. 3:27).

Into the Promised Land

Crossing the river Jordan

When Moses died, Joshua took over the leadership of the people. After sending two spies across the Jordan and into the ancient city of Jericho, he prepared the Israelites to enter the promised land of Canaan. The Ark of the Covenant (see p. 15) was taken to the head of the Israelite marching column and the people were ordered to follow the Ark, carried as usual by the Levites, across the river Jordan (Josh. 3:3–4), which dried up for their crossing.

Gilgal, the site of the Israelites' first camp on the west side of the Jordan, became their first permanent settlement, and during the early stages of the Israelite conquest of Canaan, the tabernacle was located here (Josh. 4:19; 5:10; 9:6; 10:6, 43).

Taking Jericho

The Ark figured prominently in the destruction of Jericho, being carried around the walls of the city every day for seven days, before the "great shout" on the seventh day, when the city walls fell.

After the Israelites failed to take the city of Ai, through the sin of one man, Achan, Joshua and the elders of the nation fell in front of the Ark and asked God's help.

The central sanctuary

When the Israelites had captured the central highlands of Palestine, the tabernacle was transferred there. Although the exact location is not clear, it was probably situated in turn at Shiloh, near Bethel, in the mountains of Ephraim (modern Seilun; Josh. 18:1, 10; 22:9, 12); Shechem, a city lying between Mount Gebel and Mount Gerizim, where the desert covenant was renewed (Josh. 8:30–35; 24); at Mizpah (Judges 20:1); and at Bethel (Judges 20:18, 26).

Finally the Ark was moved back to Shiloh, perhaps because of its central position, and because it belonged to the powerful tribe of Ephraim.

The tabernacle remained in Shiloh for the entire period of the judges; but the Ark of the Covenant was taken from it in the time of Eli (1 Sam. 4:4) and never returned. By the time of the prophet Samuel, the sanctuary at Shiloh, now called the "house of the Lord," appears as a more permanent structure with doors (1 Sam. 1:7; 3:3, 15; see also the Mishnah). Probably this building replaced the earlier tabernacle, which, with the passing of years and the wear and tear of moving, had

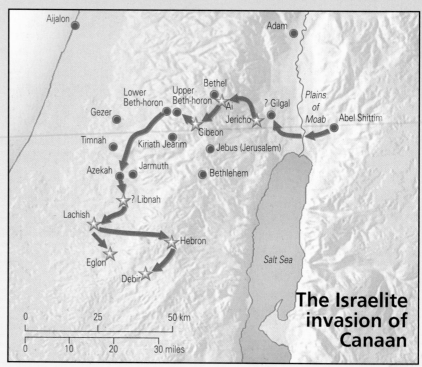

The Israelite invasion of Canaan

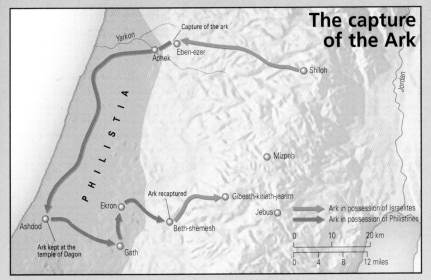

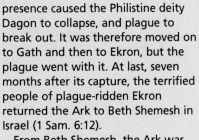

The capture of the Ark

The Philistine deity Dagon.

deteriorated. It is certainly unlikely that Moses' tabernacle survived beyond the period of the judges.

The capture of the Ark

During the time of Samuel, the warlike "Sea Peoples" or Philistines, who lived along the Mediterranean coast, threatened the existence of the Israelites. In about 1050 B.C., after a major defeat at Aphek, the leaders of Israel took the Ark into battle with them to try to compel God to fight for his people (1 Sam. 4:1–11). But the Philistines were again victorious. They captured the Ark and destroyed the sanctuary at Shiloh (as archaeologists have shown).

After the battle, the Philistines first took the Ark to Ashdod, where its presence caused the Philistine deity Dagon to collapse, and plague to break out. It was therefore moved on to Gath and then to Ekron, but the plague went with it. At last, seven months after its capture, the terrified people of plague-ridden Ekron returned the Ark to Beth Shemesh in Israel (1 Sam. 6:12).

From Beth Shemesh, the Ark was sent to Kiriath Jearim, above the modern village of Abu Ghosh, only eight miles from Jerusalem, where it was kept for twenty years (1 Sam. 7:1–2). Here Eleazar looked after it in his own house.

King David's tabernacle

When David became King over all Israel, he made Jerusalem his capital city. Here, on Mount Zion, next to his palace, he set up a new tabernacle for the Ark.

In his first attempt to bring the Ark to its new home, David did not observe the scriptural instruction for it to be carried on priests' shoulders, but transported it in a cart. When the oxen stumbled, Uzziah held the Ark to steady it, and was killed for his lack of reverence (2 Sam. 6:1–7).

Frightened by this disaster, David now stored the Ark for a further twenty years in the house of the foreigner Obed-Edom (2 Sam. 6:10).

The Ark was finally carried into Jerusalem on the shoulders of Levites (1 Chron. 15–16), with David dancing before it.

Other tabernacles

There are references to a tabernacle at Nob in the reign of King Saul (1 Sam. 21:1–6) and at Gibeon (1 Chron. 16:39; 21:29). In David's day the bread of the Presence (see p. 17) was kept at Nob (1 Sam. 21:1–6), implying that at least some of the tabernacle's sacred furniture was also situated there.

We know that at the close of David's reign the high place at Gibeon possessed relics from the original tabernacle, including the altar of burnt offering, which was still in use (1 Chron. 16:39; 21:29; 2 Chron. 1:3–6).

Upon its return to Israel, the Ark was kept at Kiriath Jearim for twenty years.

The Structure of the Tabernacle

The tabernacle was a tent that could be easily dismantled, transported, and assembled. It was intended as a fit dwelling place for God, and was therefore constructed from the highest quality materials, using the best human skills.

To underline its importance, the details of the tabernacle are spelled out three times in Exodus. Its specifications are recorded in Exodus 26, its construction described in Exodus 36:8–38, and its final erection in Exodus 40:16–19. The pattern of the tabernacle was given by God. To ensure that this pattern was followed, Moses was often reminded: "See that you make them according to the pattern shown you on the mountain" (Ex. 25:40).

The tabernacle itself was 30 cubits (45 feet/about 13.5 meters) long, 10 cubits (15 feet/about 4.5 meters) wide, and 10 cubits high.

It stood within a curtained courtyard, and was divided into two rooms, called the Holy Place and the Most Holy Place.

The framework
(Ex. 26:15–30)
The framework of the tabernacle was a series of upright supports linked by crossbars.

The upright supports
Each was about 10 cubits (15 feet/about 4.5 meters) long and 1.5 cubits (2.25 feet/about 0.7 meters) wide, and each was made of acacia wood overlaid with gold. Scholars once thought that they were solid planks of acacia wood, but today most accept that each support comprised two uprights joined together by horizontal struts, like a ladder. Such sections would be considerably stronger than planks of wood. They would keep their shape better and would allow the beautiful inner layer of curtains

to be seen from within the sanctuary. Each upright pole stood in a silver socket (Ex. 26:15–25).

The south and north sides of the tabernacle comprised twenty of these frames, with six more at the west end (the entrance was at the east end). On the west side were two extra corner pieces, to which the walls were attached by clasps (Ex. 26:23–25).

The crossbars
A series of five bars, also made of acacia wood overlaid with gold, passed through gold rings attached to each upright frame, reinforcing the stability and correct alignment (vv. 26–29; 36:31–34) of the three sides. The central bar on the south and north sides extended the entire length; the upper and lower ones were divided, their ends being fastened (as Josephus suggests) with dowels. They were probably made to different lengths, to avoid a break in the center.

Tent ropes
The whole structure was, presumably, kept in place with tent ropes, one end fastened to the knobs to which the tent cloth was attached, and the other end

The Tabernacle

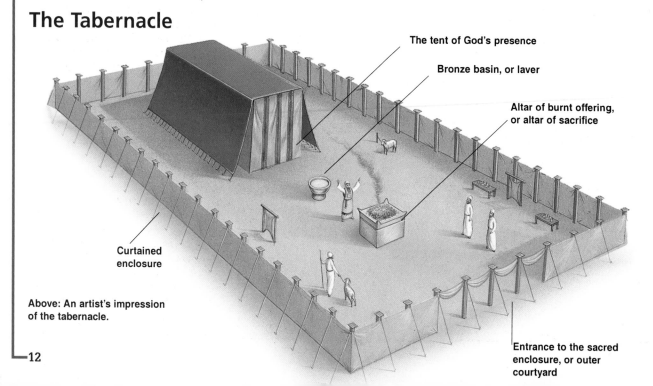

The tent of God's presence

Bronze basin, or laver

Altar of burnt offering, or altar of sacrifice

Curtained enclosure

Above: An artist's impression of the tabernacle.

Entrance to the sacred enclosure, or outer courtyard

Plan of the Tabernacle

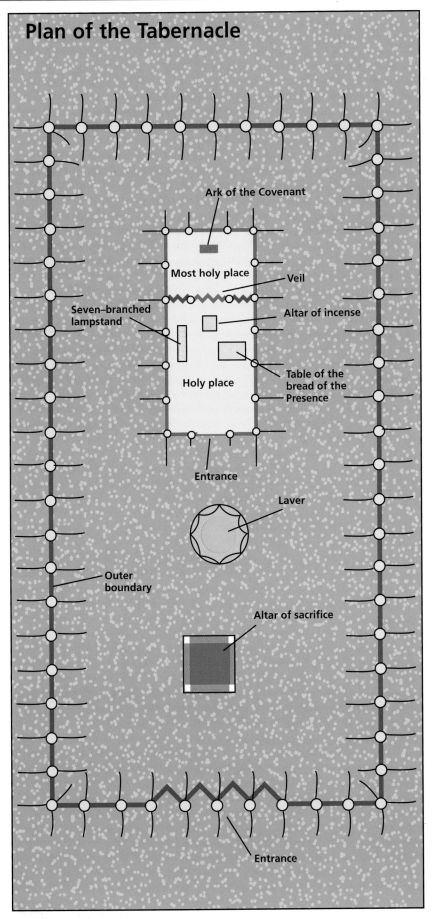

Ark of the Covenant

Most holy place

Veil

Seven-branched lampstand

Altar of incense

Holy place

Table of the bread of the Presence

Entrance

Laver

Outer boundary

Altar of sacrifice

Entrance

to brass pins driven into the ground.

The coverings
(Ex. 26:1–14; 36:8–38)
Over this framework structure four separate layers of coverings formed the top, sides, and back of the tabernacle.

The inner curtains
The inner curtains were made of linen, dyed blue, purple, and scarlet (see p. 29), and embroidered with cherubim, "worked into them by a skilled craftsman" (Ex. 36:8). There were ten inner curtains, each measuring about 42 feet (13 meters) long and 6 feet (about 1.8 meters) wide. The curtains were joined together in two groups of five, forming two covers, that were then linked together with fifty golden clasps. These clasps passed through fifty loops of blue cord to make one large cover, 28 x 40 cubits (about 42 feet/13 meters by 60 feet/18 meters).

Some scholars suggest that the curtains were suspended over a ridge pole, to prevent any sagging due to their considerable weight; but no ridge pole or supporting pillar is mentioned in the biblical description. We do not, in fact, know whether the tabernacle had a flat roof (like contemporary Phoenician shrines) or a sloping roof with a ridge pole. Probably the curtains were stretched over the structure like a tablecloth, possibly with bars fixed across the top of the tabernacle framework to take their weight and give extra strength. The embroidery could be seen only through the openings in the wooden framework inside the tent.

The second layer of curtains
Eleven curtains, or tarpaulins, of goat-hair, a loosely woven, coarse cloth, dark brown in color, formed the next layer. Each curtain was about 45 feet (about 13.5 meters) long by 6 feet (about 1.8 meters) wide. These were divided into two sets by joining together five and six curtains respectively—the

The outer door of the replica tabernacle in the Negev. *Inset*: Model of the tabernacle showing the wooden inner framework.

sixth curtain being doubled over at the east end, that is, the front of the tabernacle (26:9). The goat-hair curtains were linked together by a similar method to the linen under-curtain, except that bronze clasps were used instead of gold. Their purpose was to provide a protective covering—the Bedouin today still use goat-hair coverings for their tents. The goat hair tarpaulins were extra long, overlapping at both the front and the rear of the tabernacle, providing an overlap to protect the under-curtain (26:7–12).

The two outer layers
Two further layers ensured complete weatherproofing. One was of rams' skins dyed red and one of goat skins (v. 14). No dimensions are given for either of these covers.

The door of the tent
(Ex. 26:36–37; 36:36–37)
A screen made from the same fabric as the inner curtains stood between the Holy Place and the outer court, forming the tabernacle's eastern outer wall. It hung from golden hooks on five posts of acacia wood, covered with gold and resting in bronze sockets. There is no mention of seraphim decoration on this section, which just had simple tracery.

Inside the tabernacle
A curtain (the veil, the Hebrew word means "separation") divided the area into two compartments. Closer to the door was the Holy Place and, beyond it, the Most Holy Place.

The veil
(Ex. 26:31–33; 36:35–36)
This was a heavy, woven linen curtain made of the same material as the inner curtains. It was embroidered with cherubim—probably two cherubim, whose extended wings touched each other. Like the other hangings, it was suspended from four pillars covered with gold, with gold hooks and silver sockets at the base.

The cherubim on the veil and the curtains were symbolic guardians of the sanctuary.

The Most Holy Place
The inner room, the Most Holy Place, was the place on earth where God met with man. This room could be entered only by the high priest only once a year, on the Day of Atonement, when he sprinkled blood on the cover of the Ark of the Covenant.

The position of the veil made this room a perfect cube of 15 feet (about 4.5 meters). The layers of overlapping material, and the attention given to covering where they joined, bring home the point that it was completely dark in the innermost shrine. God was surrounded by darkness, carefully isolated from any unauthorized spectator (Ps. 97:2).

The Holy Place
The Holy Place occupied an area 30 feet (about 9 meters) by 15 feet (about 4.5 meters), exactly twice the area of the Most Holy Place. Only the priests were allowed to enter this area.

The Furniture of the Tabernacle

The Most Holy Place

Inside the ark were the two tablets of the Law, a jar of manna, and Aaron's rod.

There was distinctive furniture both in the outer courtyard of the tabernacle and within the Holy Place and the Most Holy Place.

The materials

Both precious and common materials were used to make the furniture (Ex. 25:1-7; 35:5–9). *Shittah* (plural *shittim*) wood was used widely, and comes from the acacia, or shittah, tree, rare in Israel but common in Sinai.

Three metals are mentioned, gold alone being used for the main sanctuary furnishings. Altogether, roughly one ton of gold, three tons of copper, and four tons of silver (Ex. 38:24–31) were used. The relatively large amounts of silver came from gifts freely offered by the people (Ex. 30:11–16), and this was added to the silver and gold already obtained from the Egyptians (Ex. 12:15).

The fine-twined linen of the tabernacle curtains was made from high-grade flax.

The Ark of the Covenant
(Ex. 25:10–22; 37:1–9)

The Ark was the symbol of God's relationship with his people, a relationship that was based on a promise, or contract, called the "covenant." It was therefore often called "the ark of the covenant of the LORD" (Josh. 3:3; 1 Sam. 4:3). It was also called "the ark of the Testimony" (Ex. 25:22) from the Ten Commandments (the Testimony) inside it (see "contents of the Ark" below).

The Ark of the Covenant was the only piece of furniture inside the Most Holy Place. It is significant that it was the first piece of furniture commanded to be made. However, when it came to the construction, the Ark was made after the tabernacle itself, presumably so that it could be housed immediately (Ex. 25:9; compare 36:8–37:28).

Size

The Ark was a box made of acacia wood, overlaid inside and out with pure gold. It was 2.5 cubits (approximately 3.75 feet/1.1 meters) long, and 1.5 cubits (approximately 2.25 feet/0.7 meters) wide and high (Ex. 25:10–11).

The top of the Ark

A gold rim, known in Scripture as the "crown of gold," prevented the lid, or cover, from shifting. This lid, sometimes called the "mercy seat" (NIV "atonement cover" Ex. 20:17), "a covering" (or "to make atonement") was the same size as the Ark, and was made entirely of gold. Attached to this lid were two winged cherubim, made of beaten gold. The cherubim were probably human in form, though some writers think they may have resembled the cherubim of Ezekiel 1:5–14. They were possibly of human height and are always spoken of as upright (2 Chron. 3:13). They stood facing one another, looking down onto the cover, with their wings forward and uplifted (Ex. 25:20; compare Deut. 32:11).

The inward-looking cherubim and the mercy seat formed a throne for the invisible God (Ex. 25:22), who had promised, "There . . . I will meet with you" (Ex. 25:22). He is often described as "enthroned" above, or upon, the cherubim (Ps. 80:1; 99:1), and the Ark is consequently described as God's footstool (Ps. 132:7). Like the cherubim in the Garden of Eden (Gen. 3:24), those in the Holy of Holies

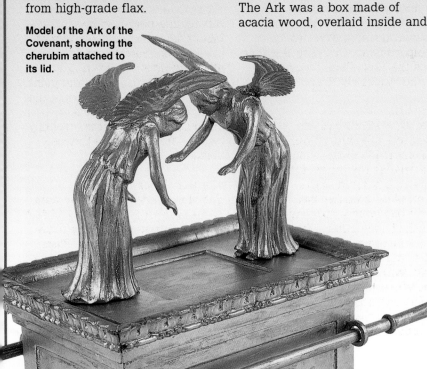

Model of the Ark of the Covenant, showing the cherubim attached to its lid.

A representation of the Ark of the Covenant carved into stonework, Capernaum.

Coin of the Jewish Revolt, representing the Ark within Herod's Temple.

31:9, 24–26), thought by some scholars to be all five books of the Pentateuch. The Ark also contained a golden jar of manna, miraculously preserved (Ex. 16:33–34) and Aaron's rod that budded miraculously, proving him to be the first high priest (Heb. 9:4; compare Num. 17:10). By the time of Solomon, however, the Ark held only the two stone tablets (1 Kings 8:9).

probably represented protectors. In the ancient world, symbolic winged creatures, such as the cherubim, were frequently positioned to guard thrones and important buildings.

The high priest sprinkled the mercy seat with blood at the climax of the annual Day of Atonement (Lev. 16:14), possibly setting down his golden censer on the lid.

Carrying the Ark

On the base of the Ark there were four gold rings, one at each corner. The Ark was carried by means of two gold-covered acacia-wood poles, each pole passing through two of the gold rings (Ex. 25:13–15). These poles were not to be removed (Ex. 25:15) unless it was necessary temporarily to remove them when the Ark was being covered (see page 23). In the Most Holy Place, the poles projected beneath the veil into the Holy Place, reminding the priests of the presence of the unseen Ark within. The Talmud (the Jewish oral law, collected and written down in the sixth century A.D.) states that these poles were 10 cubits (15 feet/about 4.5 meters) long.

The contents of the Ark

Unlike contemporary arks in neighboring countries, the Ark of the Covenant contained no representation of God. Initially, it held only the two tablets of stone on which God had written the Ten Commandments—or rather, the two tablets prepared by Moses from the originals, which he had shattered when he heard of Israel's idolatry with the golden calf (Deut. 31:18–34:29; Deut. 9:10–10:4). Also housed in or near the Ark was a copy of the Law written by Moses (Deut.

The Shekinah

Between the cherubim was the *Shekinah* (Hebrew, "residence"), the cloud in which God appeared above the cover, or mercy seat (Ex. 25:22; compare Lev. 16:2). This was not merely incense smoke (16:13). Because God was present in this cloud, no sinful person could appear before the mercy seat; even the high priest would be liable to death if he appeared before it without the atoning blood of sacrifice.

Replica of the Ark of the Covenant, showing the carrying poles.

The Furniture of the Tabernacle

The Holy Place

The outer room of the tabernacle, the Holy Place, was to be entered only by priests. It contained three pieces of furniture: a solid gold oil-fed lamp, which was the only source of light in this heavily curtained room; an altar, where incense was burnt; and a low table, on which fresh loaves of bread were placed each Sabbath.

The table of the bread of the Presence
(Ex. 25:23–30; 37:10–16)
The portable table of the "bread of the Presence" (Ex. 25:30), or showbread, was made, like the Ark, of acacia wood overlaid with gold. It was a little smaller, 2 cubits (about 3 feet/0.9 meter) long, 1 cubit (1.5 feet/about 0.5 meter) wide and 1.5 cubits (2.25 feet/about 0.7 meter) high. It

stood on the north, or right-hand, side of the Holy Place, facing the lampstand (Ex. 40:22).

The top of the table rested on a frame one hand's breadth (about 3 inches/8 centimeters) deep, around which ran a rim, with a projecting border of gold, to prevent articles slipping off the table. The table's legs were apparently fastened to the sides by means of small projections which fitted into holes. When moving the table, carrying staves were inserted through rings at each corner.

Implements (Ex. 37:16)
The various pure gold vessels for the table comprised plates for the showbread; dishes (or "spoons," KJV, and sometimes NASB) for the incense; and bowls and pitchers with a pouring spout, which, as they were used for drink-offerings, were presumably to contain wine.

The bread
Each Sabbath twelve specially prepared loaves sprinkled with frankincense—symbolizing God's provision for the 12 tribes of Israel—were placed on this table (Lev. 24:5–9). According to Jewish tradition—and as fits the dimensions of the table—the loaves seem to have been placed on plates in two piles of six each. The "bread of the Presence" placed on the table was made of fine unleavened wheat flour, baked in twelve loaves (cakes), using 0.2 ephahs (1 gallon/4.5 liters) of flour per loaf. The loaves were replaced every Sabbath with fresh loaves (1 Sam. 21:6), which had been prepared overnight by the Levites (1 Chron. 9:32). They were to be eaten solely by priests only in the sanctuary.

The seven-branched golden lampstand
(Ex. 25:31–39; 37:17–24; 40:24)
On the south (left) side of the Holy Place, opposite the table, stood the seven-branched golden lampstand (Hebrew *menorah*), the most impressive of the three

Replica of the table of the bread of the Presence. *Bottom*: The bread of the Presence.

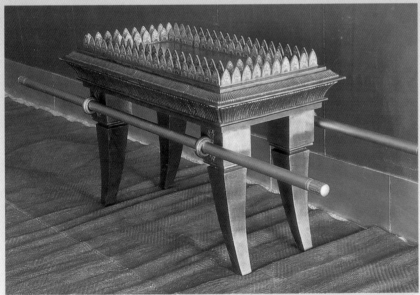

pieces of furniture in this room. Its construction is described in detail in the Bible (Ex. 25:31–40; 37:17–24), and its form is also known to us from Jewish writers and probably by a relief on the Arch of Titus in Rome.

The lampstand

Jewish tradition says that the lampstand was about 5 feet (1.5 meters) high and 3.5 feet (1.05 meters) wide. Like the cherubim and the mercy seat, it was made of pure gold; a whole talent (about 75 pounds/34 kilograms) of gold was used for the lampstand and its vessels, the various parts of it being hammered out of gold sheets.

Six golden branches, three on either side, extended from, and rose as high as, the central shaft, and probably at equal distance from one another. The lampstand's shaft rested on a pedestal, and the whole lampstand was decorated with almond flowers.

The lamps

The central shaft and all six branches ended in sockets into which were placed the seven lamps (containers for the oil, each with a wick) designed as almond-flower shaped cups, like a bud just ready to burst into bloom. It is believed that the lamps were in a horizontal line, although Exodus is not clear on this, and that the plane of the lamps ran east to west— providing optimum illumination to the Holy Place.

The oil

Only the best quality olive oil was used for the lamps, to ensure that the light was as bright as possible (Ex. 27:20). Pure or "clear" olive oil was used, prepared from olives that had been cleansed of leaves, twigs, and dust before being crushed and beaten. The resulting white oil is of the finest quality.

Above: Stone relief of a lampstand. **Below**: Replica of the seven-branched lampstand.

Lighting the lamps
The lamps were trimmed and lit at the time of the evening sacrifice (Ex. 30:8), and trimmed and filled at the time of morning sacrifice (Ex. 30:7). They are traditionally believed to have held a "log," that is a little more than a half-pint of oil.

It is not clear whether the lampstand gave continuous illumination (Ex. 27:20; Lev. 24:2) or night-time light only (Lev. 24:3; 1 Sam. 3:3, in most versions). The reference in 1 Samuel probably reflects the laxity that prevailed during the period of the judges. Without careful attention, the lights would soon grow dim, and the sanctuary be defiled by carbon deposits (Ex. 25:38).

Tools
The tools belonging to the lampstand included snuffers ("wick trimmers," NIV) and trays made of gold (Ex. 25:38), like the lampstand itself. The snuffers were used to pull up the wick to light the lamp.

The altar of incense
(Ex. 30:1–10)
The altar of incense may have been played down in order to give greater prominence to the altar of sacrifice in the outer court, which is often referred to as *"the* altar" (Ex. 30:18–20). The altar of incense was often called "the gold altar" (Ex. 40:5) to distinguish it from the bronze altar of sacrifice.

The altar of incense occupied a central space in the Holy Place, opposite the Ark, but just outside the veil, between the table of the "bread of the Presence" and the lampstand (Ex. 40:1–5).

This altar consisted of a simple square box of acacia wood completely overlaid with gold, 1 cubit (18 inches/about 0.5 meter) wide, 1 cubit (18 inches/about 0.5 meter) broad, and 2 cubits (3 feet/about 0.9 meter) high. It had horns similar to those on the altar of sacrifice and a golden moulding around the top on all four sides. This altar had no

Replica of the altar of incense, with its tools, and a mannequin dressed as high priest.

grate, because fire did not come directly into contact with it. Like the Ark, it was easily portable, and was equipped with carrying rings and poles.

Purpose
The altar of incense was used for burning incense every morning and evening. The incense, manufactured according to a special recipe (Ex. 30:34–36), could only be used in worship. The sweet-smelling smoke from the burning incense rose as a

pleasing aroma to God, symbolizing the prayers of the godly (Ps. 141:2).

The tabernacle was erected at the front edge of the western (rear) half of a large courtyard—a sacred enclosure.

The Outer Courtyard
and Its Furniture

The courtyard
(Ex. 27:9–18; 38:9–20)
The courtyard was a rectangle, 100 cubits (about 150 feet/46 meters) long on its north and south sides and 50 cubits (about 75 feet/23 meters) wide on its east and west sides.

The framework of the fence

Enclosing this space was a fence, with a framework consisting of sixty acacia wood pillars, 5 cubits (about 7.5 feet/2.3 meters) high (Ex. 27:18). The pillars were probably round, and about 5 inches (12 centimetres) in diameter, with twenty on each side and ten at each end. The base of each pillar stood in a brass socket, and each pillar was held upright by cords (Ex. 35:18) fastened to brass tent pegs (Ex. 27:19) driven into the ground, both inside and outside the court.

Curtain rods ("bands") rested on hooks near the top of the pillars, serving as the top rail of the fence, and keeping the pillars the right distance apart. These rods were made of shittim wood, covered with silver; the hooks and protecting caps on the pillars were also made of silver (38:17, 19). There were also hooks at the bottom of the pillars, to which the bottom edge of the curtains was fastened.

The curtains

Curtains of fine-twined linen (probably like modern duck) and probably white or natural in color were sewn together end to end, to form a continuous screen all around the tabernacle area. Each curtain was 22.5 feet (about 6.9 meters) long, and the curtains were 7.5 feet (about 2.3 meters) high so that no one could look over the fence.

The entrance
(Ex. 27:16–18; 38:18)

A central entrance about 30 feet (about 9 meters) wide and 5 cubits (about 7.5 feet/2.3 meters) high was located in the eastern end of the tabernacle court. The entrance was screened by an embroidered curtain woven from blue, purple, and scarlet material, and "finely twisted linen" (Ex. 38:18)—that is, the warp consisted of bleached linen threads and the woof of strips of wool dyed alternately blue, purple, and scarlet. The entrance curtain was probably set back from the fence, allowing entry at both ends. This was the only entrance into the tabernacle courtyard.

The altar of burnt offering
(Ex. 27:1–8; 38:1–7)

Anyone entering the tabernacle court immediately confronted the bronze altar of burnt offering, where sacrifices were offered to God. According to the Mosaic Law, this was the only place where sacrifices could be made. The altar stood at the east end of the court, probably about halfway between the entrance and the tabernacle itself (Ex. 40:29), reminding the people that they could not approach God except by the place of sacrifice.

The altar was a hollow box of acacia wood, 5 cubits (about 7.5 feet/2.3 meters) square by 3 cubits (about 4.5 feet/1.4 meters) high—small compared with the gigantic altar in Solomon's temple (2 Chron. 4:1). It was lined with sheets of bronze inside and out to protect it from the heat, and was light enough to be carried on bronze-covered poles that passed through bronze rings fixed at each corner.

A bronze grating or "network" (Ex. 27:4) ran around the altar,

An artist's impression of sacrifice at the altar of burnt offering.

21

Modern replica of the bronze basin, or laver, where the priests ceremonially washed.

probably halfway between the top and bottom, to create a draft and to allow the sacrificial blood to flow to the base of the altar.

At each top corner of the altar was a projecting triangular "horn," possibly symbolizing the creatures sacrificed. These horns could be used to tether the animals before sacrifice. An Israelite could claim sanctuary by clinging to the horns of the altar (see, for example, 1 Kings 1:50), perhaps because he was symbolically offering himself in sacrifice to God, and so claiming his protection.

The lower part of the altar may have been partially filled with earth, to absorb blood from the carcasses sacrificed (Ex. 20:24). The priests were not allowed to use steps to ascend the altar (Ex. 20:26); probably the earth around the altar was raised to create an inclined approach.

Implements for the altar
All the altar accessories—ash buckets, shovels for removing the ashes and filling the base with earth, basins for receiving the blood for sprinkling on the altar, pots, shovels, sprinkling bowls, meat forks, firepans or censers (Ex. 38:3; Num. 16:17)—were made of bronze (Ex. 27:3). The firepans (Ex. 27:3; "censers," Lev. 16:12) were coal-pans, used for bringing live coals from the altar.

The fire
The priests were responsible for maintaining the altar fire, which was never to be allowed to go out (Lev. 6:13). They were not to let ashes build up at the bottom of the altar, but piled them up beside the altar. Later, they took the ashes outside the camp or city.

The basin
(Ex. 30:17–20; 38:8)
Midway between the altar and the tabernacle (Ex. 30:18) stood the basin (or laver), where the priests ceremonially washed after offering sacrifices and before entering the tabernacle itself. If a priest neglected to wash at the basin before ministering he could be punished by death. No specifications concerning the shape and size of the basin have survived, but it was probably round and quite large.

A bronze pedestal supported the basin, and possibly incorporated a lower basin in which the priests could also wash their feet. Washing in the East was always done with running water, and the basin was probably supplied with taps from which the water would flow over the hands and feet of the priests. No mention is made of any other vessel in which the animal parts offered in sacrifice were washed; the basin probably served this purpose, too.

Iron shovels from Dan, used for removing ashes from the altar.

The outer fence of the replica "Tabernacle in the Desert" set up in Timna Park, Israel.

Making and Moving the Tabernacle

God's specifications for the tabernacle required skills beyond those of Moses and Aaron. Bezalel and Oholiab were in charge of the construction (Ex. 31:1–11), along with many other experts (v. 6), who presumably learned their crafts in Egypt.

The Israelites, ashamed after the incident of the golden calf (Ex. 32:1–33:6), gave so generously toward the building of the Tabernacle that the giving had to be discouraged (Ex. 35:20–24; 36:4–7). In addition to material gifts, many Israelites offered their skills (Ex. 35:25–29). To combat over-enthusiastic commitment, strict Sabbath observance was imposed (Ex. 31:12–17; 35:2–3).

Consecration

When all the furniture had been completed and placed in position within the Tabernacle (Ex. 40:1–33), everything except the mercy seat and the cherubim was anointed with special oil (Ex. 30:22–33; 40:9–11) and consecrated. Moses obeyed God in every detail of the tabernacle project (40:16, 19, 23, 25, 27, 29, 32); yet even Moses was excluded from the Holy of Holies.

Finally, the glory of the Lord filled the tabernacle (Ex. 40:34): he was among his people. After this, the cloud by day and fire by night reassured the Israelites that God was present to guide them (Ex. 40:36–38). The tabernacle was completed exactly a year after the Israelites were delivered from Egypt, and a mere nine months after the giving of the Law on Mount Sinai (Ex. 40:2, 17).

Packing up

When the tabernacle was to be moved, its dismantling was carefully regulated. Detailed directions were given for the care of the tent and its furniture (Num. 4:4–33; 7:3–9; 10:17, 21).

The sons of Kohath the Levite, known as Kohathites, were responsible for transporting the holiest objects, using the carrying poles (Num. 4:4–20). They were not, however, allowed to touch or even look at any of the holy things on pain of death (Num. 4:20). Aaron and his sons were responsible for dismantling and covering all the furniture and articles inside the tabernacle.

The Ark
(Num. 4:5–6)
The priests took down the veil and wrapped the Ark in it, to avoid its being seen by the people. Over this they placed a "porpoise skin" (NASB, KJV and NKJV; "badger skin"; NIV "sea cow"; but probably the hide of some other creature, since the porpoise was ceremonially unclean. Most writers today believe it was a specially finished covering of leather) and finally a "cloth of pure blue."

Furniture in the Holy Place
(Num. 4:7–16)
Aaron and his sons then removed the dishes from the table of showbread, spread a blue cloth over it, replaced the dishes, covered them with a scarlet cloth and "porpoise skins" (see paragraph above). The lampstand, its lamps, snuffers, and trays, were similarly covered with blue cloth and "porpoise skins," as was the altar of incense and all the other sanctuary utensils. They were then placed on biers made of two poles with crosspieces ready to be carried by the Kohathites (Num. 4:15).

The bronze altar of sacrifice
Next the great altar was cleansed of ashes, covered with a purple cloth, the altar utensils packed up in it, and covered with "porpoise skins." This work was again performed by Aaron and his sons (Num. 4:3–14).

When all these preparations were completed, the Kohathites carried the Ark and the two altars and their accessories on their shoulders.

The curtains and framework
The Gershonites were responsible for transporting all the curtains and the ropes that went with them (Num. 3:21–26; 4:21–28); and the Merarites for transporting the hard furnishings such as the frames, bars, and bases—taking them down, carrying them on the march, and fixing them when the tabernacle was set up again (Num. 3:36–37; 4:29–33).

Apart from the Ark and the altars, it seems the rest of the tabernacle was carried in six covered wagons hauled by oxen (Num. 7:3). Even on the march the tabernacle remained central, with six tribes preceding and the remaining six following (Numbers 2).

The Sacrifices of the Tabernacle

1. Burnt offerings
(Leviticus 1; 6:8–13)
This type of sacrifice was wholly burnt, except the skin, which was kept by the priests. None of it was eaten by anyone.

The worshipper brought a male animal without any defect—a bull, lamb, goat, pigeon or turtledove depending on the worshipper's wealth—to the door of the tabernacle. He then placed his hand on the creature's head to symbolize surrender to God (Lev. 1:4). The animal was then killed, and the priest sprinkled the animal's blood over the altar.

Next, the priest quartered the animal, offered its head and fat on the altar, washed the legs and entrails in water, and offered them. Any remains would be thrown into the ashes.

The burnt offering was made daily: "This is the offering made by fire which ye shall offer unto the LORD; two lambs a year old without defect, as a regular burnt offering each day" (Num. 28:3). Two animals were sacrificed each day, one in the morning and one in the evening, to atone for the people's sins (Ex. 29:38-42).

2. Cereal offerings
(Leviticus 2; 6:14–23)
The Israelites offered cereals and vegetable products as well as animals. These crops may have been offered separately from the burnt offerings, or along with them.

Leviticus 2 mentions four types of cereal offering and gives cooking instructions for each: a worshipper could offer dough from flour baked in an oven; cooked on a griddle; fried in a pan; or roasted to make bread.

All cereal offerings were made with oil and salt; no honey or leaven could be used. The worshipper also had to offer a portion of frankincense, and could bring raw grains, salt, and oil with the offering.

Worshippers brought cereal offerings to one of two priests, who took it to the altar and threw a "memorial portion" on the fire, together with all the incense. The priest ate the remainder.

The cereal offering's purpose appears to have been similar to that of the burnt offering. The offering of first fruits seems to have been intended to sanctify the entire crop. The cereal offering represented the rest of the crop, making the whole crop holy to God (Lev. 2:14).

3. Fellowship offerings
(Leviticus 3; 7:11–34)
A ritual meal called the fellowship, or peace, offering was shared with God, the priests, and other worshippers. It involved male or female oxen, sheep, or goats.

The procedure was almost identical to the burnt offering up to the point of the burning. In this case, the beast's blood was collected and poured around the edges of the altar. The fat and entrails were burned, then the rest was eaten by the priests and worshippers. This sacrifice expressed the worshipper's desire to give thanks or praise to God.

The required offerings included unleavened cakes. All but the "memorial portion" of the cakes and the remainder of the animal had to be eaten on the day of the sacrifice. When the offering was voluntary, the regulations were not so rigid.

4. Sin offerings
(Leviticus 4; 6:24–30; 8:14–17; 16:3–22)
Sacrifices for sin paid off, or expiated, a worshipper's unintentional, ritual, faults against the Lord (Lev. 4:1–2). Moses instructed various people to offer different sacrifices:

Samaritans still perform the religious sacrifice of animals on Mount Gerizim.

The Levites and priests

The Levites—members of the tribe of Levi—had a vital role in building, transporting and re-erecting the tabernacle (Ex. 38:21; Num. 1:47–51). They were not, however, allowed to serve as priests, a role reserved to Aaron's descendants. After Aaron's death, his son Eleazar became high priest (Num. 20:22).

The Levites (Num. 1:48–53)

As we have seen, each of the Levite families had special responsibilities: the Kohathites carrying the tabernacle furniture; the Gershonites looking after the coverings, screens, and hangings; the Merarites carrying and erecting the tabernacle structure.

The Levites had no particular area of land allocated to them, but were given forty-eight cities scattered throughout the Promised Land (Josh. 13:14; 21). They were supported by the peoples' tithes (Num. 18:24). Possibly later in Israel's history the strict division between priests and Levites broke down.

The high priest
(Exodus 28; Leviticus 8)
Aaron, the older brother of Moses, was made the first high priest, with his sons as priests, to minister in the tabernacle. His most solemn role—a role that could be performed only by the high priest—was to enter the Most Holy Place on the Day of Atonement to present the blood of a sacrifice for the peoples' sins. Aaron's position was confirmed when his rod budded miraculously (Num. 17).

The high priest had a special breastplate, and also carried in a pouch on his chest Urim and Thummim, through which God gave special guidance regarding his will.

The priests
The priests served between the ages of twenty-five and fifty. They were responsible for teaching God's law (Lev. 10:11); offering sacrifices (Lev. 1–4); diagnosing unclean diseases (Lev. 13:13); examining sacrifices (Lev. 22); supervising the Tabernacle (Num. 3–4); serving as judges and even going into battle.

An artist's impression of the high priest's garments.

Sins of the high priest were atoned with the offering of a bull. The blood was not poured on the altar, but sprinkled from the finger of the high priest seven times on the altar. The fat was burned next; the rest was burned outside the camp.

Sins of leaders in the community were atoned with the offering of a male goat. The blood was sprinkled only once, then the remainder was poured around the altar as in the burnt offering.

Sins of ordinary people were atoned with female animals: goats, lambs, turtledoves, or pigeons. If a person could not afford one of those, a grain offering was acceptable. The procedure for offering the grain was the same as for the cereal offerings.

A person could commit an unintentional sin in many ways. Some had moral implications; others, like those of lepers (see Luke 17:12–14), were purely ceremonial. Offerings for the nation and for the high priest covered all these in a collective way. On the Day of Atonement (Yom Kippur), the high priest sprinkled blood over the Ark of the Covenant itself. This was the ultimate atonement ritual.

5. Trespass offerings
(Lev. 5:14–6:7; 7:1–6)
The trespass offering was similar to the sin offering, and it was often included with it. However, the trespass offering was an offering of money, and was made for sins of ignorance, connected with fraud. For example, if the worshipper had unwittingly cheated another of money or property, his sacrifice had to be equal to the value of the amount taken, plus one-fifth. He offered this amount to the priest, then made a similar restitution to the former property owner. He therefore repaid twice the amount he had taken plus 40 percent (Lev. 6:5–6).

Holy Days and Festivals

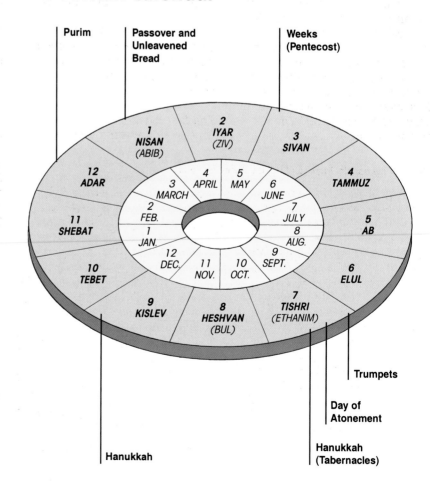

Unleavened bread is eaten at Passover.

Under Moses' leadership, the people began observing the Sabbath (Saturday) as a day for worshipping God. Every year there was also one official day of fasting (the Day of Atonement) and there were three great annual feasts: Passover, the Feast of Weeks (Pentecost), and the Feast of tabernacles (or Booths). These are often called "pilgrim feasts" because all adult males were required to travel to the sanctuary to take part (Deut. 16:16) and because they were times of joyful celebration.

The Sabbath
There seems to have been no observance of a special day of rest before the time of Moses.

Origin and purpose
The first mention of the Sabbath is in Exodus 16:23, when the Hebrews were camped in the Wilderness of Sin before they received the Ten Commandments. There God instructed them to observe the Sabbath every seven days, to allow people and animals to rest, as God rested after creating the world (Ex. 20:11; Gen. 2:2–3) and to offer thanks to God for deliverance from slavery in Egypt (Deut. 5:12–15).

Importance
Many of the laws in the first five books of the Bible concern Sabbath keeping. Breaking the Sabbath by doing any kind of work was like breaking Israel's covenant with God, and was punishable by death (Num. 15:32–36).

Offerings
Two lambs were sacrificed on the Sabbath, in addition to the daily burnt offerings (Num. 28:9–10). On the Sabbath the twelve cakes of showbread were presented in the tabernacle (Lev. 24:5–8).

Passover
(Exodus 12; Lev. 23:5) and the **Feast of Unleavened Bread** (Lev. 23:6–8)
The Passover was the first and most important of the annual feasts.

Origin and purpose
It combined two observances that were originally separate: Passover, the night celebrated in memory of the death angel's passing over the Hebrew households in Egypt; and the Feast of Unleavened Bread,

The Jewish calendar

Purim

Passover and Unleavened Bread

Weeks (Pentecost)

1 NISAN (ABIB)	2 IYAR (ZIV)	3 SIVAN
12 ADAR	3 MARCH / 4 APRIL / 5 MAY / 6 JUNE	4 TAMMUZ
11 SHEBAT	2 FEB. / 1 JAN. / 7 JULY	5 AB
10 TEBET	12 DEC. / 11 NOV. / 10 OCT. / 9 SEPT. / 8 AUG.	6 ELUL
9 KISLEV	8 HESHVAN (BUL)	7 TISHRI (ETHANIM)

Trumpets

Day of Atonement

Hanukkah (Tabernacles)

Hanukkah

A Jewish family celebrates Passover in Jerusalem.

which commemorated the first seven days of the Exodus. The two celebrations were closely linked. For example, leaven had to be removed from the house before the Passover lamb was killed (Deut. 16:4), so at the Passover meal unleavened bread was eaten (Ex. 12:8). The people of Israel eventually merged the two celebrations into one.

This great festival began on the evening of the fourteenth day of Abib (later called Nisan, our March-April) and lasted for seven days.

The first evening
On the first evening a lamb or kid was killed just before sunset (Ex. 12:6; Deut. 16:6) and was roasted whole and eaten with unleavened bread and bitter herbs. This ceremony was rich in symbolism: the blood of the animal symbolized the cleansing of sins; bitter herbs, the bitterness of bondage in Egypt; the unleavened bread, purity.

The first and seventh days of the festival were kept as Sabbaths: there was no work and the people came to a holy gathering (Lev. 23:7; Num. 28:18, 25).

On the second day of the feast, a priest waved a sheaf of the first ripe barley to consecrate the coming harvest.

Offerings
During the feast the priests daily sacrificed two bullocks, one ram, and seven lambs as a burnt offering and a male goat as a sin offering in addition to the regular sacrifices (Lev. 23:8; Num. 28:19–23).

Some of the special ingredients of the Passover meal.

The Day of Atonement, Yom Kippur, is the most solemn day in the Jewish year.

festival was the "Feast of Harvest, or Ingathering" (Ex. 23:16; 34:22).

Offerings
During the week the priest offered a burnt offering of seventy bullocks. Two rams and fourteen lambs were the daily burnt offering, and a male goat the daily sin offering (Num. 29:12–34).

Every seventh year, when there was no harvest because of the sabbatical year (every seventh year, when the land was not to be cultivated), the Law of Moses was read publicly during the feast.

The Day Of Atonement
(Yom Kippur) (Ex. 30:10; Lev. 16; 23:26–32; 25:9; Num. 29:7–11)
The Law required only one fast—the Day of Atonement.

Purpose
This day fell on the tenth day of Tishri (September–October), just before the Feast of Booths, and was devoted to the cleansing of sins. It was observed by abstaining from work, fasting, and attending a holy gathering.

Offerings
The high priest replaced his elaborate robes with a simple white linen garment and offered a sin offering for the entire nation. During the day the high priest symbolically transferred the sins of the people onto a goat (scapegoat), which was then released into the desert.

The Feast of Weeks (Pentecost)
(Ex. 34:22;
Lev. 23:15–21)
This festival was observed fifty days after the offering of the barley sheaf at the Feast of Unleavened Bread.

Purpose
The Feast of Weeks marked the end of the harvest and offering of first fruits (Ex. 23:16; Lev. 23:15–21; Num. 28:26–31; Deut. 16:9–12) and also commemorated the giving of the Law. This one-day festival was observed as a Sabbath, with a gathering at the tabernacle to thank God for the harvest. Priests urged the people to remember those in need (Deut. 16:11–12), as they did at all pilgrim festivals.

Offerings
Two loaves of unleavened bread were offered, along with ten animals for a burnt offering, a male goat for a sin offering, and two yearling male lambs for a peace offering.

The Feast of tabernacles
(Booths) (Lev. 23:33–43; Num. 29:12–40; Deut. 16:13–15)

Origin and purpose
The purpose of this festival was to remember Israel's wandering in the wilderness. It took its name from the fact that during the feast the Israelites lived in tents, or shelters (Lev. 23:40–42), as they had done in the wilderness. The Feast of tabernacles began on the fifteenth day of the seventh month (Tishri, September-October), and lasted seven days. It came at the end of the harvest season—a third name for the

On the Day of Atonement the high priest released a goat (scapegoat) into the desert.

The Symbolism of the Tabernacle

The tabernacle and its furnishings have great symbolic significance. The tabernacle showed that God is willing to meet with human beings here on earth. Both the tabernacle and the temple foreshadow the meeting of God with man in Jesus Christ.

The sanctuary of the tabernacle was called the "Tent of Meeting" between God and his people. Thus the tabernacle symbolized God's presence with his people. The glory of God filled the tabernacle, and his presence was shown to the people in the pillar of cloud and fire above it (Ex. 40:34–38; Num. 9:15–23).

Each aspect of the tabernacle had symbolic implications. For this reason Moses was told to be sure to construct it "according to the pattern shown you on the mountain" (Ex. 25:40). The New Testament emphasizes that the tabernacle was "a copy and shadow of what is in heaven" (Heb. 8:5).

General symbolism
The tabernacle is presented in the New Testament as symbolic:

1. A symbol of the church, as "a dwelling in which God lives by his Spirit" (Eph. 2:22; see Ex. 25:8);

2. A symbol of the believer who is "a temple of the Holy Spirit" (1 Cor. 6:19; compare 2 Cor. 6:16);

3. A symbol of heaven which is the true dwelling-place of God (Heb. 9:11, 23–24; Rev. 13:6).

A symbol of Christ
The furniture of the tabernacle is symbolic of Christ and his ministry.

The bronze altar
The bronze altar (Ex. 27:1–8) is symbolic of Christ's cross, where Jesus, as a "whole burnt offering," offered himself without blemish to God.

The laver
The laver, where the priests washed before entering the Holy Place or approaching the altar, symbolizes the cleansing given to the believer by Christ from the defilement of sin (John 13:2–10; Eph. 5:25–27).

The golden lampstand
The lampstand symbolizes Israel as a people called to be the children of light (Matt. 5:14) and Christ as the light of the world (John 9:5).

The table of the bread of the Presence
The table of the bread of the Presence, or showbread, symbolizes Christ as the bread of life, who sustains every believer (John 6:33–58).

The twelve cakes of showbread represented the twelve tribes of Israel dedicated to God's service.

The altar of incense
As we have seen, the altar of incense represents prayer (Ps. 141:2; Rev. 5:8). It also symbolizes Christ (John 17:1–26; Heb. 7:25), through whom our prayers rise to God (Heb. 13:15; Rev. 8:3–4).

The veil
The curtain that divided the two rooms in the tabernacle (Ex. 26:31–35) symbolizes that before Christ died there was no direct access to God (Lev. 16:2; Heb. 9:8). The tearing of the veil when Jesus died (Matt. 27:51) reflects the new reality: believers can now come to the throne of grace and find mercy and help (Heb. 4:16; 7:25).

The Ark of the Covenant
The Ark, and in particular the mercy seat, symbolized God's presence among his people. For the Israelites, it was transformed from a throne of judgement to a throne of grace by the blood of atonement sprinkled upon it. The Ark under the mercy seat symbolized to the Israelites the fact that the Law was under God's protection (Ex. 20:21).

The door
There was only one entrance into the tabernacle court, just as there is only one way by which we can come to God. Jesus said: "I am the way . . . no one comes to the Father except through me" (John 14:6).

The sacrifices
The writer of the letter to the Hebrews reveals the symbolism of the tabernacle sacrifices (Heb. 10:1–18). They were performed daily, showing that they could only cleanse a person temporarily and outwardly. But when Christ offered himself up on the cross his sacrifice was permanent, and gives inner cleansing: "By one sacrifice he has made perfect forever those who are being made holy" (Heb. 10:14).

The colors used in the tabernacle
Gold, blue, purple, and scarlet are mentioned twenty-four times in Exodus, always in that order.
• *Gold* No other metal is quite like gold. It has the greatest intrinsic value and is the purest of all metals.
• *Blue*, the heavenly color, indicates the deity of Christ.
• *Purple*, the royal color, proclaims Jesus as the King of kings.
• *Scarlet*, the color of blood, foreshadows the sacrifice of Jesus Christ on the cross for the sin of the world.

Solomon's Temple

The Tabernacle served the Israelites as a place of worship for many years. Finally, in about 1000 B.C., King David proposed building a permanent temple (2 Sam. 7:2), but Nathan the prophet told David not to, because the blood of battles was on his hands. Instead, David's son Solomon was to build the first temple in Jerusalem.

Mount Moriah, the site chosen by David for the Temple, was believed to be the place to which, centuries earlier, Abraham brought Isaac for sacrifice. Solomon's Temple was dedicated about 950 B.C. (1 Kings 6–7; 2 Chronicles 3–4). Although it was much larger than the Tabernacle, it was built to the same floorplan, and, like the tabernacle, it contained a Holy Place and Holy of Holies and the Ark of the Covenant.

Herod's Temple

Solomon's Temple stood for more than four hundred years, until it was destroyed in 586 B.C. by the invading Babylonian army (2 Kings 24:10–13). When the Persian king Cyrus encouraged the Israelites to return to Jerusalem, led by Ezra and Nehemiah, they rebuilt the city and the temple. This temple—often known as the Zerubbabel's temple—served as the focus of Jewish worship for the next few hundred years.

In 19 B.C. Herod the Great began to rebuild the derelict temple, making many fine additions. But this magnificent temple stood for less than one hundred years. Six years after its completion, in A.D. 70, it was destroyed by the Roman legions under Titus, who had been called in to quell the Jewish Revolt of A.D. 66–70. Herod's temple was the last Jewish temple to stand on this sacred site in Jerusalem.

In 638, the Muslims conquered Palestine and occupied the temple site, building the Dome of the Rock at the center of the Temple Mount in 691–2. The Temple Mount is still today controlled by the Muslims, for whom it is also a sacred place.

Authentic scale model of Herod's temple.

Index

Abraham 30
altar of incense 19, 28
altar of sacrifice 19, 21–22, 28
Ark of the Covenant 15–16
  captured by Philistines 11
  carried into Canaan 10
  rehoused by David 7
  removal 23
  symbolism 28
  what happened to it 32

Babylonia 32
basin 22, 28
Bethel 10
bread of the Presence 17
burnt offerings 24

camp around the tabernacle
  4, 8
Canaan see Promised Land
cereal offerings 24
cherubim 14, 15–16
colors 28
courtyard 20–22
covenant 15
curtains 13–14, 21
Cyrus 31

David and his temple 7, 11
Day of Atonement 14, 16, 26,
  28
Dome of the Rock 31, 32

Exodus 9
Ezekiel 5
Ezra 31

fellowship offerings 24
festivals 26–28
furniture 15–19, 23

Gershonites 23
Gibeon 7, 32

Herod the Great and his
  temple 30
high priest 25
Holy Place 17–19, 23

incense 19

Jericho 10
Jerusalem 7
Josephus 5
Joshua 6, 10
Josiah 32

Kiriath Jearim 11
Kohathites 23

lampstand 17–19
laver 22, 28

Levites 25

Manasseh 32
mercy seat 15, 16
Mizpah 10
Moriah, Mount 30
Moses 6–8, 16, 23
Most Holy Place 14, 15–16
Muslims 31

Nehemiah 31

Passover 26–27
peace offerings 24
Pentecost 28
priests 22, 25
Promised Land 10

Sabbath 26
sacrifices 24–25, 28
sanctuary 7
Shechem 10
Shekinah 16
Shiloh 10
sin offerings 24–25
sins 25
Sinai, Mount 6, 8, 9
Solomon and his temple 5, 29

Tabernacle
  forerunner of the temple 4
  how we know about it 5
  location in Palestine 10
  Mount Sinai 6
  permanent structure in
    camp 8, 12–13
  plan 13
  removal 23
  symbolism 28
Tabernacles, Feast of 28
temple
  meaning of the word 7
Temple Mount 31
Ten Commandments 16
tents 4, 6
trespass offerings 25

veil 14, 28

Yom Kippur 28

Zerubbabel's temple 31

What Happened to the Ark?

The Gibeonite shrine continued to be used until the time of King Solomon (1 Kings 3:4, 5; 1 Chron. 16:39), but the sacred furniture surviving from Moses' tabernacle was transferred to Solomon's temple at Jerusalem (1 Kings 8:4), which was conceived as a "place of rest for the ark of the covenant of the LORD" (1 Chron. 28:2). Solomon's Temple was built on Mount Moriah, today the site of the Dome of the Rock on the Temple Mount in the Old City of Jerusalem. The Ark was placed in darkness in the Holy of Holies within the temple sanctuary, and its staves removed, as it had finally arrived at its resting place. The temple incorporated everything that remained of the earlier tabernacle worship, and the history of the tabernacle ended at this point (1 Kings 8:4). This is the final reference to the tabernacle in the Old Testament.

During the reign of King Manasseh, a graven image was set up in the Temple, and possibly the Ark was taken into hiding by the Levites (2 Chron. 33:5; 35:3). It was restored by King Josiah, but we read nothing more of it. It is not listed as being plundered by the Babylonians at the fall of Jerusalem (2 Kings 25:13–17); nor is it pictured as being looted by the Romans on the Arch of Titus after the destruction of Jerusalem in A.D. 70.

Where is the Ark?
A Hebrew tradition says that, when Babylon captured the city of Jerusalem, the Ark of the Covenant was taken from the Temple by Jeremiah and hidden in a cavern (2 Macc. 2:1–8). Some people believe it is in Axum, Ethiopia. Many rabbis believe the Ark is hidden beneath the Temple Mount. The legend runs that the Ark's hiding place has never been found, and never will be, until Messiah establishes his kingdom and restores Israel's glory.

Some rabbis believe the Ark of the Covenant is hidden beneath the Dome of the Rock.